NAME YOUR EMOTIONS

SOMETIMES I FEEL LONELY

by Lakita Wilson

PEBBLE
a capstone imprint

Published by Pebble, an imprint of Capstone.
1710 Roe Crest Drive, North Mankato, Minnesota 56003
capstonepub.com

Library of Congress Cataloging-in-Publication Data
Names: Wilson, Lakita, author.
Title: Sometimes I feel lonely / Lakita Wilson.
Description: North Mankato, Minnesota : Pebble, an imprint of Capstone, 2022.
| Series: Name your emotions | Includes bibliographical references and index. | Audience: Ages 5-8 | Audience: Grades K-1 | Summary: "What does it mean to be lonely? Loneliness may not make us feel good, but it's an emotion everybody has! Children will learn how to identify when they are lonely and ways to manage their feelings. Large, vivid photos help illustrate what loneliness looks like. A mindfulness activity will give kids an opportunity to explore their feelings"—Provided by publisher.
Identifiers: LCCN 2021029773 (print) | LCCN 2021029774 (ebook) | ISBN 9781663972323 (hardcover) | ISBN 9781666326031 (paperback) | ISBN 9781666326048 (pdf) | ISBN 9781666326062 (kindle edition)
Subjects: LCSH: Loneliness—Juvenile literature. | Emotions—Juvenile literature.
Classification: LCC BF575.L7 W55 2022 (print) | LCC BF575.L7 (ebook) | DDC 158.2—dc23
LC record available at https://lccn.loc.gov/2021029773
LC ebook record available at https://lccn.loc.gov/2021029774

Image Credits
Capstone Studio: Karon Dubke, 5; Getty Images: Image Source, Cover, Juanmonino, 15; Shutterstock: Africa Studio, 13, anek.soowannaphoom, 19, fizkes, 17, GOLFX, 9, Iakov Filimonov, 12, mirjana ristic damjanovic, 21, Monkey Business Images, 11, Prostock-studio, 7, vichie81, 6, Winai Tepsuttinun, 21 (jar)

Editorial Credits
Editor: Erika L. Shores; Designer: Dina Her; Media Researcher: Jo Miller; Production Specialist: Tori Abraham

Printed and bound in the USA. PO4608

TABLE OF CONTENTS

Words in **bold** are in the glossary.

WHAT DOES IT MEAN TO BE LONELY?

Imagine everyone in your family is too busy to chat. Your friends are too busy to play. You go into an empty room, and there's nothing but quiet. Today, everyone is too busy to hang out with you. You are probably feeling lonely. Loneliness is an **emotion**, or feeling.

WHAT DOES IT FEEL LIKE TO BE LONELY?

Being lonely doesn't always mean you are alone. Maybe you feel like people have forgotten about you. You might feel like no one cares. You might crave **attention** from the people you love most.

You might become **clingy**. Maybe you ask people to play with you over and over. Sometimes loneliness causes you to act in unusual ways. You might cry or act out.

USING YOUR SENSES

Everyone has five **senses**. People can touch, taste, smell, see, and hear things. Your senses send messages to your brain. It's where feelings start. Everyone feels lonely at times.

Seeing a photo of a friend who moved away might make you feel lonely. Hearing other kids playing while you are alone in your room can too.

TALKING ABOUT YOUR FEELINGS

Keeping lonely feelings inside can make you feel worse. Talk about your feelings with someone you trust. Talking can help you understand what is causing you to feel lonely. Maybe a grown-up can help you think of things to do on your own. Maybe a friend can suggest a game to play together.

UNDERSTANDING LONELINESS

Even though it doesn't feel good, loneliness doesn't last forever. It often helps to understand why you feel this way. Being left out of a game might make you feel lonely. An argument with a friend can make you feel all alone.

Other emotions can lead to loneliness too. Maybe you are sad that a pet died. You might remember the fun you had together. This can leave you feeling lonely.

HANDLING YOUR FEELINGS

Being lonely can make you act differently. You might lose interest in doing the things you usually like to do. You might **mope** around. You might even cry. You start to question if your loved ones still care about you. It's important to know how to deal with these feelings.

There are things you can do to feel less lonely. You can make a list of people who care about you. You can also list ways these people show they care.

Share your lonely feelings with one of the people on your list. You can talk to them in person. Or you can write them a note or call them.

You can help others who are lonely too. Introduce yourself to a classmate who sits by themselves at lunch. Have you noticed a kid who doesn't talk much to other kids? Invite them to sit and play with you. Showing kindness helps everyone feel less lonely.

MINDFULNESS ACTIVITY

Try this activity when you feel lonely.

What You Do:

1. Find an empty jar. Make sure it's clean and dry.

2. Decorate your jar using art supplies like paint, glitter, glue, and stickers.

3. Next, cut 10 strips of paper.

4. On each paper strip, write something you like to do by yourself. For example, "color" or "read."

5. Place each paper strip into your jar.

The next time you feel lonely, take out one of the strips. Do the activity you wrote down. Your loneliness will melt away.

GLOSSARY

attention (uh-TEN-shuhn)—notice, interest, or awareness

clingy (KLING-ee)—staying very close to someone

emotion (i-MOH-shuhn)—a strong feeling; people have and show emotions such as happiness, sadness, fear, anger, and jealousy

mope (MOHP)—to wander around in a state of unhappiness or boredom

sense (SENSS)—a way of knowing about your surroundings; hearing, smelling, touching, tasting, and sight are the five senses

READ MORE

Braxton, Simone. *Sometimes We Feel Lonely.* New York: Cavendish Square Publishing, 2022.

Morey, Allan. *When Your Friend Is Lonely.* Minneapolis: Jump!, Inc., 2020.

Stratton, Connor. *I Feel Lonely.* Mendota Heights, MN: Little Blue House, 2021.

INTERNET SITES

KidsHealth: Talking About Your Feelings

kidshealth.org/en/kids/talk-feelings.html

PBS Kids: Feelings Games

pbskids.org/games/feelings

INDEX

ABOUT THE AUTHOR

Lakita Wilson writes books for children. She loves to read, put together jigsaw puzzles, and travel. She lives in the Washington, D.C., area with her two children and grumpy old dog, Gus.